POSTCARDS
FROM HEAVEN
BY CLAIRE CLONINGER

*his book is lovingly dedicated
to Curtis, my firstborn,
who sees like a prophet and loves like a servant,
and to Andy, my prodigal,
whose faith is a light to the lost.*

POSTCARDS FROM HEAVEN

BY CLAIRE CLONINGER

WORD PUBLISHING

Dallas · London · Vancouver · Melbourne

POSTCARDS FROM HEAVEN
Messages of Hope, Courage, and Comfort from God's Heart to Yours

All Scripture quotations are from *The Holy Bible, New Century Version,* copyright © 1987, 1988, 1991 by Word Publishing, Dallas, Texas 75039.
Published in association with the literary agency of Alive Communications, P.O. Box 49068, Colorado Springs, Colorado 80949.

Library of Congress Cataloging-in-Publication Data

Cloninger, Claire
    Postcards from heaven : messages of hope, courage, and comfort from God's heart to yours / by Claire Cloninger.
       p.   cm.
    ISBN 0–8499–0975–9
    1. Consolation.   I. Title.
    BV4905.2.C56   1992
    242—dc20   92–17824
                                                                 CIP

Printed in the United States of America

2 3 4 9 BMG 9 8 7 6 5 4 3 2 1

Table of Contents

Early in my Christian walk, someone told me that the Bible was a love letter from God to his people. I've never forgotten that. I can hardly think of a crisis in my life, little or large, from that time to this, when I haven't gone to the Word of God for comfort, guidance, and strength. And I've never come away empty-handed.

Many times when I've needed a touch from the Lord, he has led me to a particular verse or passage. Years ago I learned to "personalize" those special messages, to rephrase them as from God's heart directly to me.

For instance, I might personalize a verse like "My God will use his glorious riches in Christ Jesus to give you everything you need" (Phil. 4:19) like this: *Dear Claire, I am in the process of taking care of your problem. I know exactly what you need, and I intend to supply that need from my glorious storehouse of riches in Christ Jesus. Your loving Father, God."*

I began to think of these "personalized" Scripture verses as "postcards from heaven." What power they have had over the years to alter my attitude and increase my faith!

Several summers ago, while I was attending a church conference in the mountains of North Carolina, the Lord led me to send one of these "postcards from heaven" to my friend Toni, who was going through a tough time. It was then that I discovered their power to minister to others.

From childhood, Toni's life had been a series of losses and tragedies. Although she was happily married to a wonderful man, there were places of pain in her past that she had never dealt with. The result? At some subconscious level, Toni was furious at God. But being a "good Christian," she was having trouble acknowledging that, even to herself.

It was during one of the conference workshops on inner healing that Toni began to recognize her anger. She stayed after the teaching to confer with the workshop leader, a wise young pastor who suggested that Toni go back to her cabin and spend as much time as she needed writing a very honest letter to God. He assured her that God already knew her true feelings but that he wanted her to be willing to acknowledge and express them herself.

"God prefers your honest anger to a veneer of false acceptance any day," the workshop leader told Toni. "You can't have a real love relationship with someone you're not being honest with. And that's the only kind of relationship God is interested in having with his children."

Toni wrote the letter. In the heart-wrenchingly honest words of a wounded child, she poured out the pain of a lifetime. She released her feelings of abandonment and let her anger rage. She pleaded with God to help her understand all that she had been through so that she could accept it and go on. Then she delivered the letter, not to the gates of heaven, but to my cabin!

"Would you be God for me?" she asked me timidly. "I feel like I'm writing into a vacuum. I mean, I know he's there, but it would help me to have somebody read the letter and let me know it's okay."

I read that letter and I wept. Then I prayed.

"Lord," I asked, "what can I say to Toni? Help me tell her that you love her. Help me show her how you feel toward her. Show me what you would say to her, Lord, if you were here in person to take her in your arms and comfort her."

Suddenly a flood of Scripture began to flow into my mind. Verses of wisdom and comfort and courage began to surface. It was as though the Lord was reminding me of all the words he had *already* spoken to Toni (and all the Tonis who have ever been wounded by the world). This is the "postcard from heaven" that the Lord led me to write to my friend:

Dear Toni,

I got your letter. I read every word, and I understand. There are so many things I want you to know. You are my child—precious to me. When you are hurting, I hurt, too. When this fallen and imperfect world wounds one of my children, I am wounded, too.

Do you know that I am right here beside you? I always have been, and I always will be. I will not leave you comfortless. When you walk through the dark valley, I will be with you. You must open your eyes of faith and use them to see me in the midst of your situation. I am here, and I'm on your side. I want you to keep talking to me. Cast every care of your heart upon me, because I care for you. Do not give way to panic. I will keep your heart and mind in perfect peace. Walk with me. Let me be your God. Your husband cannot be your God. Neither can your friends. I have given you these special people to care for you and help you. But no human being can ever be to you who I am. I am your God. Let me prove myself to you. Lean on me. Call on me. I am here for you. I love you. You are my own.

Your Father for all time,

God

In a magnificent mountain setting, Toni read her "postcard from heaven." Only she and God know exactly what happened as she read. But she later confided to me (and to our Monday night Bible study group) that a new phase of trust and communication began that day between herself and God. She said that though the words she read hadn't answered all of her questions, they had showed her the Father-heart of God. And that was the beginning of healing in her relationship with him.

I know that the words of the "postcard" had power in Toni's situation because they were from God's heart. Each attitude and emotion expressed on God's behalf is directly traceable to his character as revealed in the Bible. (Later I gave Toni a list of Bible verses to look up which clearly showed that the God of the Bible and the God of the "postcard" are one and the same! These Scriptures are Ephesians 1:17-21; Philippians 4:6-7; Matthew 11:28-30; Deuteronomy 33:27; Jeremiah 29:11-13; Jeremiah 31:3; Romans 8:31-39; John 14:1, 18, 27; and Hebrews 13:8.)

God is trying to communicate with each of us every day in every situation of our lives. His care and concern for every one of our problems is very personal and individual. The Holy Spirit is longing to minister the good news of God's Word to every pain, need, concern, or area of confusion in our lives. (It's no accident that Jesus urged us to pray to God as "Abba"—the Hebrew equivalent of "Daddy.")

Postcards from Heaven is a collection of "personalized" messages from the heart of God to each believer who is ready to move into a more personal love relationship with him. Every "postcard" brings a message of hope or help or healing, of comfort, courage, or consolation. (Each one is printed along with Scripture references to authenticate its origin.)

Not only are these messages wonderful to receive into our own lives, they are also wonderful to share with others who are needing a word from God. As you read, you may find a particular "postcard" that would encourage your sister or your neighbor or your child. That is when you will discover, as I did, a joyful new way of giving away God's good news!

Claire

I WILL HEAL YOUR WOUNDS

Heavens and earth, be happy.
   Mountains, shout with joy,
because the Lord comforts his people
   and will have pity on those who suffer. . . .
The Lord answers, "Can a woman forget the
     baby she nurses?
   Can she feel no kindness for the child to
     which she gave birth?
Even if she could forget her children,
   I will not forget you.
See, I have written your name on my hand."

Isaiah 49:13, 15–16

Lord, you have examined me and know all
     about me.
You know when I sit down and when I get up.
   You know my thoughts before I think them.
You know where I go and where I lie down.
   You know thoroughly everything I do.
Lord, even before I say a word,
   you already know it.
You are all around me—in front and in back—
   and have put your hand on me.
Your knowledge is amazing to me;
   it is more than I can understand.

Psalm 139:1–6

Dear child of mine,
look back on the years of your growing up, and my eyes can see
all the times and situations in which you were hurt, whether
intentionally or unintentionally. I can hear the wounding words
and see the harmful deeds, and I know the scars you carry in your
personality because of them. Sometimes the very people you looked to for love and
affection were the ones who wounded you most. Sometimes they were members of
your own family!

But hear me now, my child. Though they have wounded you, I will never wound
you. Though they have let you down, I will never let you down. Though their words
and deeds have harmed you, I speak to you words of hope and healing. I reach out to
you with justice and kindness and love. I am constantly thinking of you, my child.
You are always with me. I cannot forget you for one moment. See, I have written your
name on the palms of my hands. Come now and let me heal the wounds of your
childhood.

Your loving Abba,
God

I MADE YOU FOR A REASON

The Lord spoke his word to me, saying:
"Before I made you in your mother's womb,
 I chose you.
 Before you were born, I set you apart. . . ."

Jeremiah 1:4–5

You made my whole being;
 you formed me in my mother's body.
I praise you because you made me in an
 amazing and wonderful way.

Psalm 139:13–14

My dear child,

I *created you for a purpose. There is a specific reason for your life. You are important to me. When circumstances or people in your life make you feel insignificant, remember that you are of great value and significance to me. I knew who you would be before you were even born. While you were still in the womb, I was putting you together according to my own design. I formed you exactly as you are.*

Don't you see? I didn't make any mistakes when I made you. You are wonderfully made! I am filled with pride over you, my precious one! Be at peace with yourself. I love you as you are.

You are you. You are mine!

Love,
God

I Will Wait for You

"So the son left and went to his father.
"While the son was still a long way off,
his father saw him and felt sorry for his son.
So the father ran to him and hugged and
kissed him. The son said, 'Father, I have
sinned against God and have done wrong to
you. I am no longer worthy to be called your
son.' But the father said to his servants,
'Hurry! Bring the best clothes and put them
on him. Also, put a ring on his finger and
sandals on his feet. And get our fat calf and
kill it so we can have a feast and celebrate.
My son was dead, but now he is alive again!
He was lost, but now he is found!'"

Luke 15:20–24

Dear child,

ou *think you understand my love. But I wonder. Do you know just how much I love to be with you? Do you know how much I miss you when you're gone? You can turn your back on me and walk away; I'll wait for you. You can move to a foreign country; I'll watch the road for your return. You can ignore my wishes and wander from my ways. You can make the wrong choices and listen to the wrong voices and waste every treasure I've placed in your hands. Still my ear will listen for your knock on the door.*

Is it you? I will wonder, and my heart will leap. Is it my child at last? And on that day when I see you from a long way off, weary and broken and headed for home, I will rush out to meet you. I'll cover your shame with a cloak of righteousness. I'll cook a meal and call my friends and plan a celebration. And as I look into your face, which is so dear to me, tears will fill my eyes, and I will say, "My child was lost, but now is found! My child was dead, but now is alive again!"

With open arms!

God

I Am the One You Need

"Just as I was with Moses, so I will be
with you. I will not leave you or forget you."

Joshua 1:5

The Lord says, "I am the one who comforts
    you.
  So why should you be afraid of people,
    who die?
  Why should you fear people who die like
    the grass?"

Isaiah 51:12

Dear child,

aven't you learned by now where your comfort comes from? Haven't you discovered the wellspring of your joy and the source of your strength? I am the God who comforts you. I am the Friend who brings joy.

Why do you continue to look to the people in your life for things that can only come from me? I have given you special people to enjoy and care about. I have given you people to learn from and people to nurture. But these are human beings like yourself. Though they may never intend to, there will come a time when they will let you down. If you continue to go to them for the fulfillment that can only be found in me, a time will come when you are left empty and alone. A time will come when the people you relied on will reveal that they are only human.

My love is a higher love. It is a love you can trust. I will not leave you nor forget you.

Total fulfillment will not come from others. Being totally "full-filled" means being filled full of my Spirit. Come and be fulfilled in me.

Your Father and your Friend,
God

THERE IS NO NEED TO GO ON LIKE THIS

"But I planted you as a special vine,
    as a very good seed.
How then did you turn
    into a wild vine that grows bad fruit?"

Jeremiah 2:21

"I am the vine, and you are the branches.
If any remain in me and I remain in them,
they produce much fruit. But without me
they can do nothing. If any do not remain in
me, they are like a branch that is thrown
away and then dies. People pick up dead
branches, throw them into the fire, and burn
them. If you remain in me and follow my
teachings, you can ask anything you want,
and it will be given to you."

John 15:5–7

16

My dearest child,

I t breaks my heart to see the way you struggle and struggle in your own strength. So often you feel depleted. You push and fret and end up feeling burned out and alone. There is no need for you to go on like this. I long to give you inner strength. Draw on my resources and live as you were designed to live—as a branch attached to the vine of my eternal love. All that you require will flow from my abundance to your need. And when my life has filled your emptiness to overflowing, it will branch out into the lives of those around you. I am the vine; you are the branch. Come to me and live.

Abundantly yours,
God

I Am Here for Your Hurt

"He will not break a crushed blade of grass
    or put out even a weak flame
until he makes justice win the victory."

Matthew 12:20

When Jesus heard them, he said, "It is
not the healthy people who need a doctor,
but the sick."

Matthew 9:12

My dear child,

re you hurting today? Under all the coping mechanisms you've set up to keep your life in motion, is there a place in you that is bruised and aching, a hidden place in need of healing?

I know. I can see. I want to heal you. It is to the downtrodden and the broken that I come. Let me in. Don't hide the wounded places. Don't show me only the shiny achievements and the competent areas of your life. I am here for the hurt in you, too. I want to bring health to every part of you. I want to see you flourish. I want to make you whole. So when the wick of your candle is smoldering and almost out, cry out to me. I will send the gentle wind of my Holy Spirit to stir up that flame of life in you.

Compassionately yours,
God

Don't Give Up!

So we do not give up. Our physical body
is becoming older and weaker, but our spirit
inside us is made new every day. We have
small troubles for a while now, but they are
helping us gain an eternal glory that is much
greater than the troubles. We set our eyes
not on what we see but on what we cannot
see. What we see will last only a short time,
but what we cannot see will last forever.

2 Corinthians 4:16–18

Dear child,

Do not give up. Do not feel defeated or hopeless or down on yourself. It's true that the outward circumstances of what is happening look grim to you. It's true that the world feels dreary and dismal tonight, and you feel tired. But don't dwell on the outward things, on your physical surroundings or the particulars of this situation. These outward things are actually in the process of deteriorating and passing away right before your eyes.

Your lifetime on this planet only lasts a moment. But you yourself are eternal. You are forever because your real life is in me and I am in you. Your body may be aging, but your spirit is "youthening"! As you dwell in me, your spirit person is being vitalized and energized and given new vision.

All the piddling trivia you're wrestling with is but a blink of my eye. All the difficulties and heartaches you're struggling with are already in the process of being formed by my hand into a glory that is beyond your comprehension—a glory that is eternal. So don't keep your eyes glued to the frustrations or the heartaches; lift your eyes to me. See me with your spirit and believe my voice within you now. I am more real than anything your eyes can see. I am more powerful than anything your hands can touch. I am more lasting than anything your senses can perceive.

I am real life!

God

You Cannot Change My Love

This is what real love is: It is not our love for God; it is God's love for us in sending his Son to be the way to take away our sins.

1 John 4:10

But God shows his great love for us in this way: Christ died for us while we were still sinners.

Romans 5:8

You have been saved by grace through believing. You did not save yourselves; it was a gift from God. It was not the result of your own efforts, so you cannot brag about it.

Ephesians 2:8–9

Dear child of mine,

A s you were growing up in this imperfect world, you learned that if you were a good little child, you would be loved. This is the kind of love the world is famous for. It is called "conditional love" because it comes with conditions—with strings attached. It is love you must work and strive and struggle to earn. But it is not real love. It is a counterfeit—a cheap forgery of a priceless masterpiece.

My love is real and unconditional. It cannot be earned. Try to understand this truth, for it will deeply affect the way you live your life: *You cannot make me love you more by anything you do or do not do. And you cannot make me love you less by anything you do or do not do.*

Take a minute and read those two sentences again. If you are willing to allow my deep, true, unconditional love to seep down into your wounded spirit, that love will make you whole. And from the endless stream of love I shall put within you, true repentance will flow. Then you will live a good life, not in order to make me love you, but because I already do love you! You will be set free to live with joy and abandon. You will be released to love others with this same kind of love.

Does it sound too good to be true? Dare to believe it. Open your heart to receive it. You will never be the same.

Unconditionally,
God

WHAT IS YOUR ANSWER?

Then Jesus asked, "But who do you say I am?"

Peter answered, "You are the Christ."

Mark 8:29

My child,

here is one question that you alone can answer. When it is put to you, answer carefully. Your reply must flow from the inmost depths of who you are. No authority on earth can help you answer, and no authority on earth can refute your true response. Your answer to this one question will determine the way you live your life. It will mold your character and chart your course. It will be both your anchor and your compass. And it will move for you the very gates of eternity.

"Who do you say I am?" Jesus asked Peter. When that question is put to you, I pray your reply will be, "The Christ, the Son of the living God. My Lord and my King."

Be ready to answer.
God

I Will Meet You There

Also, the Spirit helps us with our weakness. We do not know how to pray as we should. But the Spirit himself speaks to God for us, even begs God for us with deep feelings that words cannot explain.

Romans 8:26

Lord, listen to my words.
   Understand my sadness.
Listen to my cry for help, my King and my God,
   because I pray to you.
Lord, every morning you hear my voice.
   Every morning, I tell you what I need,
   and I wait for your answer.

Psalm 5:1–3

My dear child,

rayer is not complicated. It is very simple. It is a conversation between your heart and mine. It is a place where all of your questions and all of my answers can find each other. It is the breath of my Holy Spirit cooling your anxiety and stirring up the flames of your faith. It is a time for you to reflect on who I am, and a time for me to strengthen and comfort who you are.

Don't worry about prayer. Don't intellectualize about prayer. Don't study prayer. Just pray. You will learn to pray by praying. When you don't know where to start, start with praise. When you don't feel worthy, repent and receive my forgiveness. When you don't know what to say, don't struggle. My Spirit knows how to express the deep longings of your heart apart from your words.

Come needy. Drink deeply. Praise freely. Be filled.

I will meet you there.

God

I DELIGHT IN THE ORDINARY

Your beauty should come from within you—the beauty of a gentle and quiet spirit that will never be destroyed and is very precious to God.

1 Peter 3:4

In all the work you are doing, work the best you can. Work as if you were doing it for the Lord, not for people. Remember that you will receive your reward from the Lord, which he promised to his people. You are serving the Lord Christ.

Colossians 3:23–24

Dear child,

ou look for great ways to bring me glory. You feel frustrated and somehow stuck in the ordinary things of life. Know this: I delight in the ordinary. I delight in a life lived simply and obediently before me. When you choose to embrace the small struggles and simple pleasures of this one day, you honor me. You cannot offer higher praise to me than the praise of a calm and joyous life. Do each small task as an offering to me, for I see and appreciate your work. Enter into each conversation with a determination to let my words come out through you, for I hear and delight in such conversation. In this way, the most common life becomes extraordinary. The simplest day becomes holy.

I am with you in this ordinary day.
God

LEAN INTO MY MERCY

"Don't be afraid, because you will not be ashamed.
   Don't be embarrassed, because you will not be
      disgraced.
You will forget the shame you felt earlier;
   you will not remember the shame you felt when
      you lost your husband.
The God who made you is like your husband.
   His name is Lord All-Powerful.
The Holy One of Israel is the one who saves you.
   He is called the God of all the earth.
You were like a woman whose husband left her,
   and you were very sad.
You were like a wife who married young
   and then her husband left her.
But the Lord called you to be his,"
   says your God.

Isaiah 54:4–6

My dear and precious child,

*D*o you know that when you weep, I am weeping with you? Do you know that your wounds wound me and your heartaches break my heart?

Do not be afraid. You are not alone; I am here. Do not fear disgrace, for I will stand up for you in your humiliation. Whatever pain or shame or reproach you have felt in your life, I desire to redeem it and make it right.

I am your God. The Lord Almighty is my name. I am the Holy One of Israel, your Redeemer. Confide in me, lean into my mercy, trust the strong arm of my righteousness. I will stand up for you.

Mightily and mercifully yours,
God

I Will Do It

Now may God himself, the God of peace, make you pure, belonging only to him. May your whole self—spirit, soul, and body—be kept safe and without fault when our Lord Jesus Christ comes. You can trust the One who calls you to do that for you.

1 Thessalonians 5:23–24

My dear one,

ou spend tremendous energy on trying to be a good Christian. But self-effort will never produce the completed saint. Instead, spend that same amount of time and effort just sitting at my feet. Read my Word. Listen to my voice. Absorb my truth. Let the lifeblood of my gospel begin to flow through your veins, and you will begin to be remade. A person will most surely become like those with whom he or she keeps company. Trust me. I am faithful, and I will never ask of you what I am not willing to perform in your life.

I will do it!

God

I AM ALWAYS THERE

Where can I go to get away from your Spirit?
    Where can I run from you?
If I go up to the heavens, you are there.
    If I lie down in the grave, you are there.
If I rise with the sun in the east
    and settle in the west beyond the sea,
even there you would guide me.
    With your right hand you would hold me.
I could say, "The darkness will hide me.
    Let the light around me turn into night."
But even the darkness is not dark to you.
    The night is as light as the day;
    darkness and light are the same to you.

Psalm 139:7–12

Dear one,
our life is filled with so many things—so many people and plans
and places and appointments. You rise early, and you go to bed
late. And though you may stop and turn to me briefly, in only a
moment you are off again into your own thoughts and
imaginations and pursuits.

Do you think that I am part of one world and not of another? Do you think that I
am the God of prayers and church and not the God of business and relationships?
Don't you know that there is no place you can go apart from my Spirit—that my
presence goes with you always?

If you go up to heaven, I am there. If you sink to the depths, I am there also. If
you fly to the far side of the ocean, I am still there. There is no darkness so deep that
my light cannot penetrate and dispel it.

Oh how I long for the time when you will welcome me into every boardroom and
living room, every conference and conversation. I want to be your confidant. I want to
be your closest friend.

I want to be your
God

YOUR SOUL WILL DELIGHT IN ABUNDANCE

The Lord says, "All you who are thirsty,
   come and drink.
Those of you who do not have money,
   come, buy and eat!
Come buy wine and milk
   without money and without cost.
Why spend your money on something that is not
    real food?
   Why work for something that doesn't really
    satisfy you?
Listen closely to me, and you will eat what is good;
   your soul will enjoy the rich food that satisfies."

Isaiah 55:1–2

Dear child of my heart,

o you sometimes feel caught on a treadmill? You wake and you work and you worry. You stop and you sleep and you start all over again. Are you following dreams that are not my dreams and plans that are not my plans? Why do you spend your money on obsessions that only make you restless for more? Why spend your energy on things that will never satisfy that inner hunger in you? I created you with a longing that only I can fill. "All you who are thirsty, come and drink. Those of you who do not have money, come, buy and eat."

Listen to me, trust in me, reach out to me, and your soul will delight in the richness of spiritual abundance.

Your own,
God

I Am Drawing Good from Bad

We know that in everything God works for the good of those who love him. They are the people he called, because that was his plan.

Romans 8:28

Dearest child,

Everything in your life can be used as a part of my plan for good. Yes, even the bad things. Even the very situation that you think is intolerable or hopeless or unredeemable. Trust me. This thing, too, will work together for your good and my glory.

How is that possible? It is possible because you love me, because you have been called to walk in my ways, and you have answered yes to that call. Even now I am in the process of drawing good from the bad. I am committed to taking whatever evil comes into your life and bringing good out of it.

All things will work together for good. Not just some, but all. Even your own failures and faults and areas of sin are opportunities for me to work. Commit them to me. Confess them. Put them under the blood of my Son. Even these things will give you cause to praise me.

Trust me in this.
God

Do Not Fall in Love with the World

Do not love the world or the things in the world. If you love the world, the love of the Father is not in you. These are the ways of the world: wanting to please our sinful selves, wanting the sinful things we see, and being too proud of what we have. None of these come from the Father, but all of them come from the world. The world and everything that people want in it are passing away, but the person who does what God wants lives forever.

1 John 2:15–17

But the Spirit produces the fruit of love, joy, peace, patience, kindness, goodness, faithfulness, gentleness, self-control.

Galatians 5:22–23

Today I ask heaven and earth to be witnesses. I am offering you life or death, blessings or curses. Now, choose life! Then you and your children may live.

Deuteronomy 30:19

My dearest child,

The world holds out to you a surface sort of happiness that depends on favorable circumstances. But I hold out joy.

The world offers relationships fraught with hidden agendas and self-serving motives. I offer love, gracious and unconditional.

The world holds out blame and shame and condemnation. I hold out forgiveness and the road to a new beginning.

The world rewards you with addictions and compulsions and momentary gratification. But I will fill you with peace that passes understanding.

The world offers broken contracts, vows, and promises. I give you my Word, that never changes.

The world runs hot and cold. One day you're valued and respected; the next you're forgotten like yesterday's headlines. But my character is love, and I am the same yesterday, today, and forever.

Oh, my child, do not fall in love with the world. It holds out to you only an imitation of life. I hold out life, abundant and free.

Choose life!

God

LEAVE TOMORROW IN MY HANDS

"Don't worry and say, 'What will we eat?' or 'What will we drink?' or 'What will we wear?' The people who don't know God keep trying to get these things, and your Father in heaven knows you need them. The thing you should want most is God's kingdom and doing what God wants. Then all these other things you need will be given to you. So don't worry about tomorrow, because tomorrow will have its own worries. Each day has enough trouble of its own."

Matthew 6:31–34

Dearest child,

here are two ways you can go about the business of your life. You can be stressed and anxious and crippled with worries. Or you can trust that I am in control, working in your circumstances, and you can be free!

Why is trust so difficult for you? Why do you worry about menus and calories and grams of fat? Why do you fret about styles and fashions and pulling together the right wardrobe? Life is so much more than food. Your body is so much more important than the clothes you put on it every morning.

Look up. See the birds? They have never made a grocery list or counted a calorie, and yet they are fed. Find a field filled with flowers. Spend an hour gazing at their beauty. Do you think they are worried about what's in style this year or what color goes with what? Now, if I take care of birds and flowers, can't you believe that I will take care of you? It is the godless person who worries about these things. But you are my own child. Seek my kingdom, and I'll provide for you. Leave tomorrow in my hands.

I love you.
God

I'll Give You the Right Words

Then the Lord said to him, "Who made a person's mouth? And who makes someone deaf or not able to speak? Or who gives a person sight or blindness? It is I, the Lord."

Exodus 4:11

"When you are brought into the synagogues before the leaders and other powerful people, don't worry about how to defend yourself or what to say. At that time the Holy Spirit will teach you what you must say."

Luke 12:11–12

My own child,

Trust me today for the words you need to say. Rely on me, and I will supply you with the right words for every situation. Dwell in me, and I will dwell in you. Dwell in the wisdom of my Word, and my wisdom will dwell in you.

Then, when you are called upon to speak, you will know what to say. The words will come from your heart—words of comfort or words of confrontation, whatever you need. Whatever situation arises, you will be able to go to the well of my wisdom and draw from the living water of my Word.

Be bold! I am with you, now and always.

Your Strength and Supply,
God

I Want to Tell You a Secret

"Be careful! When you do good things, don't do them in front of people to be seen by them. If you do that, you will have no reward from your Father in heaven.

"When you give to the poor, don't be like the hypocrites. They blow trumpets in the synagogues and on the streets so that people will see them and honor them. I tell you the truth, those hypocrites already have their full reward. So when you give to the poor, don't let anyone know what you are doing. Your giving should be done in secret. Your Father can see what is done in secret, and he will reward you."

Matthew 6:1–4

Dearest child,

I want to tell you a secret. I want to show you a path of joy. I want to open a door for you that leads to blessing. The key to that door is marked "giving." And not merely "giving," but "giving without expecting any reward or praise from other people."

When you give secretly to others without expecting them to reward you, I will reward you with a quiet inner joy. When you do your good deeds, expecting no fanfare from people, there will be great fanfare for you in heaven.

Trust me, my child. Think today of some need that you can meet in secret. Then go about meeting that need in a quiet and thankful way. I will be with you. And we will rejoice together!

Generously,
God

I Am Closer Than Your Heartbeat

"Be quiet and know that I am God."

Psalm 46:10

"I leave you peace; my peace I give you.
I do not give it to you as the world does. So
don't let your hearts be troubled or afraid."

John 14:27

My dearest child,

I am calling you into a place of rest, into a haven of stillness. The world can be a tyrant, pushing and rushing and driving you. You need not yield to its merciless rhythms. I will give to you a peace that the world cannot give or comprehend. I will place my peace within you. I will draw you to me out of the rush and confusion and will teach you to enter my rest.

Though the world swirls about you like a mad whirlpool, my Spirit at the center of your being is a fountain of stillness and peace. There, I am closer than your heartbeat. There, you can be still and know that I am God.

Enter my rest. There you will know me.

I am . . .

God

CONSIDER THE GIFTS

Who says you are better than others?
What do you have that was not given to you?
And if it was given to you, why do you brag
as if you did not receive it as a gift?

1 Corinthians 4:7

They knew God, but they did not give
glory to God or thank him. Their thinking
became useless. Their foolish minds were
filled with darkness. They said they were
wise, but they became fools. . . . They
traded the truth of God for a lie. They
worshiped and served what had been
created instead of the God who created
those things, who should be praised
forever.

Romans 1:21–22, 25

Dearest child,

Today as you go about your work, consider the gifts you have been given. Think of the talents and abilities I have formed in you which enable you to do your job.

You may say to yourself, "I have been trained or educated to do these things." But think about it. Where did you get the intelligence with which you reason and learn, the talent with which you create, the reflexes which allow you to develop skills? You could not have been educated without these gifts.

It is tempting at times to allow your work to become a subtle kind of idol in your life. Remember when you are in the midst of toiling, laboring, creating, and earning that I, the Lord your God, am a jealous God. Do not worship the work of your hands, but worship the One who has equipped you to do the work.

Sovereignly,
God

When You Have Fallen Short, Look to Jesus

All have sinned and are not good enough
for God's glory.

Romans 3:23

Those who heard Jesus began to leave one
by one, first the older men and then the
others. Jesus was left there alone with the
woman standing before him. Jesus raised up
again and asked her, "Woman, where are
they? Has no one judged you guilty?"
She answered, "No one, sir."
Then Jesus said, "I also don't judge you
guilty. You may go now, but don't sin
anymore."

John 8:9–11

Dear child,

When you have sinned and fallen short of my glory, believe me, you are in the company of great Christians everywhere! "All have sinned and are not good enough" for my glory—there are no exceptions.

I know how devastating sin can be to everyone it touches. That is why I sent my perfect Son into the world as an offering for sin. When you have fallen short, look to him.

How did he deal with the fallen men and women of his day? Once a woman caught in adultery was brought before him. He heard her accusers, who wanted to stone her. And the first thing he did was get rid of them!

(If Satan has become your accuser, trying to destroy you, speak out the name and the truth of Jesus, and he must back off! If he insists on reminding you of your past, remind him of his future! Remind him of Calvary and the empty tomb. Remind him whose heel is now upon his head! That should shut him up!)

After getting rid of this woman's accusers, Jesus lifted her to her feet and spoke to her words of affirmation and healing. Then he lovingly sent her off, telling her to sin no more. In short, he restored her. And that is what he wishes to do for you. Don't remain in the devastating aftermath of your sin. Go to Jesus now.

Lovingly,
God

Don't Look Back

I do not mean that I am already as God wants me to be. I have not yet reached that goal, but I continue trying to reach it and to make it mine. Christ wants me to do that, which is the reason he made me his. Brothers and sisters, I know that I have not yet reached that goal, but there is one thing I always do. Forgetting the past and straining toward what is ahead, I keep trying to reach the goal and get the prize for which God called me through Christ to the life above.

Philippians 3:12–14

Child of mine,

This journey we are on together is forward looking. The destination is ever before you. You have not arrived, but you are on your way. Press on. Take hold of that glorious purpose for which Jesus Christ has taken hold of you. His purpose is that you know him, that you become like him, that your life become a channel through which his love can flow to others. His purpose is that you spend eternity enjoying me, starting now!

Many have traveled this road before you, and you can learn from them. Consider Paul. Suppose he had taken time out from his journey to dwell on past failures. He could have looked back and become paralyzed by the guilt and shame of a life spent persecuting the church of Jesus Christ. Why, Paul even held the coats of the murderers who stoned my servant Stephen! He stood by watching in approval. But once he was forgiven, Paul did not waste time or spiritual energy looking back. He knew that the past had been put under the blood of Jesus, and he was free to press on toward the goal.

Do you know these things about your past? Come be forgiven, once and for all, and then look back no more. Instead, look ahead to the glory that lies out before you. And press on!

God

Be Strong in Me

Finally, be strong in the Lord and in his great power. Put on the full armor of God so that you can fight against the devil's evil tricks. Our fight is not against people on earth but against the rulers and authorities and the powers of this world's darkness, against the spiritual powers of evil in the heavenly world. That is why you need to put on God's full armor. Then on the day of evil you will be able to stand strong. And when you have finished the whole fight, you will still be standing.

Ephesians 6:10–13

God did not give us a spirit that makes us afraid but a spirit of power and love and self-control.

2 Timothy 1:7

Dearest child,

*T**here's a battle raging all around you this very day. You cannot see the enemy with your human eyes, for this fight is in the spirit realm, against forces of evil. The enemy soldiers take their orders from the Prince of Darkness, the unseen power who controls this world.*

Does all this sound like some sort of a scary story made up to frighten you? Believe me, it is not; these things are real. You need to be warned. But you do not need to be afraid. Not ever. I have not given you a spirit of fear, but a spirit of power and love and self-control. I have provided for your defense and your protection. I am even sending you out as a warrior to stand against this enemy of mine.

No longer are you to be weak and ineffective. Instead, be strong! Your strength will not come from yourself, but from me. I have boundless resources of power. So put on my full suit of spiritual armor, and you will surely be able to resist the enemy and to stand for me through every trial and temptation.

Your Commander-in-Chief,
God

You Will Find Me

"Ask, and God will give to you. Search, and you will find. Knock, and the door will open for you. Yes, everyone who asks will receive. Everyone who searches will find. And everyone who knocks will have the door opened."

Matthew 7:7–8

"You will search for me. And when you search for me with all your heart, you will find me!"

Jeremiah 29:13

Then God said to Moses, "I AM WHO I AM. When you go to the people of Israel, tell them, 'I AM sent me to you.'"

Exodus 3:14

Dear child, *am not difficult to find. I am not trying to elude you or hide myself from you. I am here, and when you are ready to find me, you will. You will find me when you seek me with all that you are. When you are through playing intellectual games and spiritual hide-and-seek. When you stop trying to create me in your image. When you stop giving me ultimatums and deadlines and telling me how God should act.*

When it's really me that you want and not some deity of your own design, then you will surely find me. My name is I AM—the God of power and majesty, the God of justice and mercy. I am Jehovah—the God of the garden, the flood, the wilderness, and the mountaintop. I am Abba—the God of Jesus, the God of the cross and the grave, the Resurrection and the Life. Seek me; you will find me.

I AM WHO I AM.

God

Turn Around . . . Now

You belong to your father the devil, and you want to do what he wants. He was a murderer from the beginning and was against the truth, because there is no truth in him. When he tells a lie, he shows what he is really like, because he is a liar and the father of lies.

John 8:44

My dear children, I write this letter to you so you will not sin. But if anyone does sin, we have a helper in the presence of the Father—Jesus Christ, the One who does what is right. He is the way our sins are taken away, and not only our sins but the sins of all people.

1 John 2:1–2

"Change your hearts and lives because the kingdom of heaven is near."

Matthew 3:2

Dear child of mine,

o you've slipped and somehow fallen back from your commitment to me. And now the enemy is trying to tell you that you're really not a Christian, that you'll never make it and you might as well give up. But consider the source. Satan is a liar. He would love to see your life bounce right back into his court.

Would it interest you to know what I think of your situation? Would it surprise you to know that your sin never surprises me? I understand human beings. I thought them up! And I understand sin. That is why I have made a flawless provision for it. That provision is the blood of my own Son, Jesus Christ. His part was painful and costly so that your part could be simple. Your part is to repent.

To repent is not to sit around being morosely sorry about what you've done— though you probably will feel sorry. To repent is not to mope around, beating yourself up for your failure—though you may feel that you deserve it. To repent simply means "to turn around." It is a decision word, an action word, not a feeling word. Your feelings can't help you now; it's time to act.

Repent. Turn around. Change your heart and life. Confess, be forgiven, and come home. Do it now!

I'm waiting . . .
God

Pull the Root of Bitterness

Try to live in peace with all people, and try to live free from sin. Anyone whose life is not holy will never see the Lord. Be careful that no one fails to receive God's grace and begins to cause trouble among you. A person like that can ruin many of you.

Hebrews 12:14–15

When they came to a place called the Skull, the soldiers crucified Jesus and the criminals—one on his right and the other on his left. Jesus said, "Father, forgive them, because they don't know what they are doing."

Luke 23:33–34

My dear child,

id someone who should have been a friend turn out to be an enemy? Has your surprise turned to hurt? Has your hurt turned to righteous indignation and your indignation to anger? Can you now feel that anger putting out little roots of bitterness that will dig into the soil of your tender heart and hold tight? Let me help you now, my child. For bitterness will not only poison your life, but it will ruin many other people. Whatever pain you are in, however much you feel you have been wronged, pull up that bitter root before it takes over and spoils the spiritual climate of your whole life.

My Son stands beside you. He lives within you. More than anyone, he understands what it is like to be betrayed, denied, mocked, and wronged. And yet, listen to his haunting words. Let them echo down the caverns of your pain: "Father, forgive them, because they don't know what they are doing."

Can you say these words in your situation? Only my Son can give you the grace and the power to do so.

Let him do it.
God

Your Thoughts Are Valuable

We destroy people's arguments and every proud thing that raises itself against the knowledge of God. We capture every thought and make it give up and obey Christ.

2 Corinthians 10:4–5

Accept God's salvation as your helmet, and take the sword of the Spirit, which is the word of God.

Ephesians 6:17

Dearest child,
our thoughts are valuable, for they determine to a great degree what your actions will be. My enemy is constantly fighting to gain some control in your life, and his first line of attack is always your mind. He knows that to gain control of your thoughts is to gain control of your actions.

But you are not to fear, for the victory is mine. I have given you every protection you will need. I have placed upon your head a special helmet that protects your mind and its every thought. It is called "the helmet of salvation" because it covers every thought in your mind with the protective reality of your standing in my kingdom. Now, when the enemy's lies begin to fly like arrows, you will recognize them for what they are. Your thoughts will abide in the truth of my Word, and your mind will rest in the reality of who you are in Christ.

You are a sinner saved by grace. You are my precious child. Your knowledge of this truth will allow you to "capture every thought and make it give up and obey Christ."

As your thoughts become more Christlike, they will lead you to act with mercy and compassion and wisdom, just as Christ would. As your mind embraces my truth, you will become like my Son.

Think on him and his love.
God

I Have Equipped You Fully

Then I said, "But Lord God, I don't know how to speak. I am only a boy."

But the Lord said to me, "Don't say, 'I am only a boy.' You must go everywhere I send you, and you must say everything I tell you to say. Don't be afraid of anyone, because I am with you to protect you," says the Lord.

Jeremiah 1:6–8

My child,

can see that you are struggling with feelings of inadequacy. You are not feeling equipped to do all that you must do today. I'm asking you to remember this one thing when the circumstances of your day threaten to discourage you. Remember that I will never ask you to do anything for which I have not first equipped you. You can trust me on that! You can step out, fully confident, knowing that I am with you. Don't be afraid or intimidated by the people who oppose you. I, the Lord your God, am with you. I will supply your adequacy.

Faithfully,
God

You Will Be Satisfied

Those who want to do right more than anything else are happy, because God will fully satisfy them.

Matthew 5:6

"He must become greater, and I must become less important."

John 3:30

My dearest child,

ou are blessed indeed when you are hungry and thirsty for me, for you will be satisfied; you will be filled. Be thankful when you find yourself yearning for more of me—more guidance, more courage, more comfort, more company. The deep longings in your spirit for me will most surely be answered.

Nothing is more compelling to my Holy Spirit than a sincere heart that longs for me and my righteousness. To "long for my righteousness" is to yearn for a right relationship with me. And what is a right relationship? One in which you become so infused by and empowered with my Holy Spirit that you bear the mark of my character to all who know you. This is what it means for you to "become less important" so that I may "become greater."

Hunger and thirst for me.

God

I MEAN IT FOR GOOD

Then Joseph said to them, "Don't be afraid. Can I do what only God can do? You meant to hurt me, but God turned your evil into good to save the lives of many people, which is being done."

Genesis 50:19–20

Child of mine,

ave you been accused of a wrong by a friend or a brother? Are you inwardly writhing under the sting of that accusation? Have a million rationales in defense of your innocence begun to organize themselves in your mind?

If your heart is already becoming cold toward your accuser, stop now before you miss what I have for you in this situation. For even though he or she may have intended to harm you, I mean to bring good out of this for you. All that comes to you can be used for your growth and my glory if you submit to it.

Slow down now. Prayerfully clear your heart of malice and defensiveness. Consider the charge. Strip it of the emotionally charged language and see the bare bones of it. Before you take another breath, be brutally honest before me.

Is there any scrap of truth about the accusation, however small? (Avoid the phrase "yes, but . . . ") Remember, you are not responsible for the other person's wrongdoing in the situation. I will hold him or her accountable. You are only responsible for your own wrongdoing.

Whatever you have found that needs to be confessed, do so now—to me and to that brother or sister. My forgiveness is here for you. Let me help you bridge that gap and mend that relationship. Come clean. Be forgiven and at peace. Be reconciled.

Your Father,
God

I HAVE GLORIOUS PLANS FOR YOU!

"I say this because I know what I am planning for you," says the Lord. "I have good plans for you, not plans to hurt you. I will give you hope and a good future."

Jeremiah 29:11

God knew them before he made the world, and he decided that they would be like his Son so that Jesus would be the firstborn of many brothers.

Romans 8:29

Dear child of mine,

Today the future may look bleak or shadowy to you. But, oh, if you could only see what glorious plans I have for you, you would be rejoicing! These are plans to prosper you and bring you joy, not to hurt you nor humiliate you. All that I have planned has been motivated by my deep love for you.

Do not fret nor worry about every little detail of my plans right now. They will not be revealed to you today. But as you trust and walk with me one step at a time, I will reveal them to you. Each day you will know what you need to know. And this much I can tell you today: The purpose of my plan is that you be shaped and molded into the very image of my Son. That is the high calling of your life. So hold on through the darkness and trust me. I hold you in the hollow of my hand. Nothing comes to you without passing through the strong right hand of my righteousness. All is well.

Your faithful Father,
God

I Want First Place in Your Life

Those things were important to me, but now I think they are worth nothing because of Christ. Not only those things, but I think that all things are worth nothing compared with the greatness of knowing Christ Jesus my Lord. Because of him, I have lost all those things, and now I know they are worthless trash. This allows me to have Christ.

Philippians 3:7–8

Then God spoke all these words: "I am the Lord your God, who brought you out of the land of Egypt where you were slaves.
"You must not have any other gods except me."

Exodus 20:1–3

Dear child,

Of what are you proudest in your life? What pursuits bring you the most joy? What things really define who you are?

Whatever these things are (your family, your career, your friendships, even your service to me), offer up thanks for them, for they are a gift. And then, gratefully, move them into second place.

Every good thing in your life must come second to the best thing in your life. First place must be reserved for knowing me. What you once considered profit, now consider loss compared to the joy of knowing me. Whatever was valuable, now consider it trash compared to the joy of walking with me.

I am speaking here of priorities. I am not saying you should despise your family or your work or your ministry. But I am saying that knowing me must mean more to you than any of these. For I love you with a jealous love. I will not share that prime place in your affection with anything, however good. Loving me must be the passion that defines your life.

Should you be asked, "Who are you, and what do you do?" what would you answer? Would you say, "I am a mother," or "I am a computer analyst," or "I preach the gospel of Jesus Christ"? All of these are second-place answers. Instead, I would have you answer, "I am the beloved child of the most high God, whom I delight to know."

Jealously yours,
God

Here's How to Show Your Love

My children, we should love people not only with words and talk, but by our actions and true caring.

1 John 3:18

"Free the people you have put in prison unfairly
    and undo their chains.
Free those to whom you are unfair
    and stop their hard labor.
Share your food with the hungry
    and bring poor, homeless people into your
        own homes.
When you see someone who has no clothes, give
        him yours,
    and don't refuse to help your own relatives.
Then your light will shine like the dawn,
    and your wounds will quickly heal.
Your God will walk before you,
    and the glory of the Lord will protect you from behind.
Then you will call out, and the Lord will answer.
    You will cry out, and he will say, 'Here I am.'
The Lord will always lead you.
    He will satisfy your needs in dry lands
    and give strength to your bones.
You will be like a garden that has much water,
    like a spring that never runs dry."

Isaiah 58:6–9, 11

Dear child,

ou have told me that you love me, and you long to prove your love. But how? you wonder. What do I desire of you? Will I be impressed with lofty words or fasts or sacrifices? No. Here is the way to show me your love. Here is the way to my heart. Break the chains of injustice. Stand for the oppressed. Free those around you who are in bondage. Welcome strangers. Share your food with the hungry, and open your home to those who have no place to go. And don't get so busy helping the needy that you forget your own family. Love your wife, your husband, your parents. Listen to your children, and let them know they are important to you. When you do these things, then you will feel my pleasure and share my delight. For your light will break forth like the dawn, and all that is sick in your own soul will be healed. You will call me, and I will answer. I will continually guide you. I will satisfy your deepest needs and strengthen you. And you will be like a well-watered garden, like a spring whose waters never fail.

To show your love for me, love others.
God

COME, BE RENEWED

Surely you know.
    Surely you have heard.
The Lord is the God who lives forever,
    who created all the world.
He does not become tired or need to rest.
    No one can understand how great his
      wisdom is.
He gives strength to those who are tired
    and more power to those who are weak.
Even children become tired and need to rest,
    and young people trip and fall.
But the people who trust the Lord will
      become strong again.
They will rise up as an eagle in the sky;
    they will run and not need rest;
      they will walk and not become tired.

Isaiah 40:28–31

My precious one,

The world you live in is obsessed with staying young. Every day you see people around you spending enormous amounts of time and energy and money on any scheme that promises to keep them youthful. Some have mastered the art of looking young on the outside while their spirits within them are withered and old. They are tired of the uphill struggle of their existence and bored with its routines; they hunger for something more. Above the roar and the rumble of their stressful lives I am calling them, saying, "Surely you know. Surely you have heard. I am the Lord, the God who lives forever, the Creator of the ends of the earth. I give strength to the weary and power to the weak. Everyone who chases this world's vain pursuits will grow weary and old. But those who hope in me will renew their strength. They will soar like eagles. They will run and not need to rest. They will walk without growing tired."

Come to me and be renewed.

God

Someone Understands

Since we have a great high priest, Jesus the Son of God, who has gone into heaven, let us hold on to the faith we have. For our high priest is able to understand our weaknesses. When he lived on earth, he was tempted in every way that we are, but he did not sin. Let us, then, feel very sure that we can come before God's throne where there is grace. There we can receive mercy and grace to help us when we need it.

Hebrews 4:14–16

Who can say God's people are guilty? No one, because Christ Jesus died, but he was also raised from the dead, and now he is on God's right side, begging God for us.

Romans 8:34

Dear child,

Sometimes you feel that no one understands what you are going through. Even those closest to you don't seem to comprehend or care. I want you to know today that you are not alone. For I have given you more than a Savior, more than a distant and ethereal high priest who exists above all human experience. I have given you a friend who has walked through this human life before you.

How well he understands your breaking heart! How well he knows what it is to be beaten back by fatigue, plagued by enemies, misunderstood by friends. Whatever you are struggling with today, he has struggled with that same emotion or feeling. Whatever your temptation, he was tempted that way, too. Wherever your feet are on the journey, his footprints are in the road ahead of you.

Never again do I want you to say that no one understands. Jesus Christ understands, and because he sits at my right hand day and night interceding for you, I am constantly being reminded of your plight. I encourage you, my child, to come into my presence with boldness and confidence. Tell me what's going on. I have mercy for your sins and grace to uplift you when you're hurting.

You see, I understand, too.

God

OPEN YOUR CLENCHED FISTS

Lord, you are great and powerful.
　　You have glory, victory, and honor.
　　Everything in heaven and on earth
　　　belongs to you.
The kingdom belongs to you, Lord;
　　you are the ruler over everything.
Riches and honor come from you.
　　You rule everything.
You have the power and strength
　　to make anyone great and strong.

1 Chronicles 29:11–12

The earth belongs to the Lord,
　　and everything in it—
　　the world and all its people.

Psalm 24:1

Dear child of mine,

*Y*ou take great pride in your ownership of certain things. You fret and worry over your money and how you will spend it, your work and how you will be compensated for it, your possessions and how to protect them. How much more peaceful you will be once you have come to the realization that everything you "own" is really owned by me. All that you "possess" is actually on loan to you for a season. Your things, your money, your family, your job, even the gifts and talents that allow you to do your job—all of these are mine.

I have given you stewardship over these things for a time. Enjoy them. Be thankful for them. Use them well. But do not worry over them, for they are my concern. You can trust them to my care.

So when you wake up tomorrow morning, as you dress for work, think how best you can honor me as you go to **my** job! As you write a check, ask me how I would have you disperse **my** money! As you pray for your family, say, "Father, these loved ones of mine are really **yours**. Give me the wisdom and compassion to love them for you!" Open your clenched fists and put the control of your life and your possessions back where it belongs. In my hands.

Trust me.

God

ALWAYS BE THANKFUL!

Always be joyful. Pray continually, and give thanks whatever happens. That is what God wants for you in Christ Jesus.

1 Thessalonians 5:16–18

Dear child,

When good things come into your life, come to me and give thanks. When financial and material blessings come to you, give thanks. When you wake on an autumn morning, and the air is cool and filled with promise, and your eyes are amazed by the awesome beauty of my creation, give thanks to me. When your loved ones are gathered close and your heart is filled with the joy of their company, give me thanks.

But when trouble comes, when questions crowd your mind, when those close to you have let you down, when the skies turn dark and help seems far away—what then?

Then, too, give me thanks. Know that I am in control. Thank me, knowing that in spite of what you see with your eyes, I am working my will in every situation. That I have promised never to leave you nor forsake you. That I love you and am very near—nearer than your tears and nearer than your trouble.

In good times, your thanks will flow from a heart of gratitude. In difficult times, your thanks will flow from a heart of faith. But at all times, give me thanks.

Your faithful Provider,
God

LISTEN WITH YOUR LIFE

My child, pay attention to my words;
    listen closely to what I say.
Don't ever forget my words;
    keep them always in mind.
They are the key to life for those who find
        them;
    they bring health to the whole body.
Be careful what you think,
    because your thoughts run your life.

Proverbs 4:20–23

Scripture is given by God and is useful
for teaching, for showing people what is
wrong in their lives, for correcting faults,
and for teaching how to live right. Using the
Scriptures, the person who serves God will
be capable, having all that is needed to do
every good work.

2 Timothy 3:16–17

Dear child,

Before you open my Word this morning, stop and consider what you are holding in your hands. It is more than paper and ink, more than words and sentences. You are holding in your hands the very essence of who I am! My Word is my nature, my wisdom, my guidance, my love distilled into letter form. You are holding health and life, truth and healing. Keep my Word before your eyes. Give it permission to roam the rooms of your heart—cleaning, straightening, rearranging; closing doors on some things, opening windows on others. My Word can be for your heart a companion, a hearth, and a housekeeper; a gardener to weed your thoughts and a guard against intruders. And so, as you open my Word this day, read with your eyes, but listen with your life.

I want to speak to you.

God

Your Work Is Not My First Concern

Don't you believe that I am in the Father and the Father is in me? The words I say to you don't come from me, but the Father lives in me and does his own work. . . . I tell you the truth, whoever believes in me will do the same things that I do. Those who believe will do even greater things than these, because I am going to the Father.

John 14:10, 12

Dear child,
watch you laboring and fretting and anxiously striving to achieve
things for me and my kingdom. Hear me. Your work is not my
primary concern. Your work is now, has always been, and always
will be secondary to your relationship with me.

What you do will flow out of your relationship with me as irrigation streams flow out of a deep, clear, powerful river. The river (the relationship) will set your motives and supply your strength. Then your work will flow forth to honor me. Any time you allow your work to come ahead of your relationship with me, you risk working against me and my purposes.

Draw near to me and rest. Seek my will at every small turn. Listen for my voice. Be filled with my Spirit. Then work with joy and abandon!

The Source of your power,
God

Get a Grip! Stand Steady!

Our fathers on earth disciplined us for a short time in the way they thought was best. But God disciplines us to help us, so we can become holy as he is. We do not enjoy being disciplined. It is painful, but later, after we have learned from it, we have peace, because we start living in the right way.

You have become weak, so make yourselves strong again. Live in the right way so that you will be saved and your weakness will not cause you to be lost.

Hebrews 12:10–13

My child,

Someday you'll look back at what you're going through now with a different perspective. Every adult who has come out of a loving and nurturing home can remember trying times in his or her childhood. Nobody's childhood is all fun and games. At some point the ideas of the child and the ideas of the parent will be in conflict. But a parent who operates out of love is strong enough to make the hard calls, whether or not those decisions make for happiness at the time.

The important thing is the ultimate result. What kind of adult is this child going to become? And though the discipline of our youth is never really pleasant, in retrospect we are often able to see what it was about. This will be true in your spiritual life as well. When my purposes are accomplished, you will look back at these tedious and painful times and see what I was doing in your life. If you accept this time prayerfully and obediently, you will be able to watch the fruit of real goodness grow up in you because of it.

So get a grip! Stand steady! Don't wander off, but stay close to me and forge ahead! The foot that stays on the right path will not stumble.

I love you!
God

Speak a Blessing to Someone

The words I told you are spirit, and they give life.

John 6:63

"If you want good fruit, you must make the tree good. If your tree is not good, it will have bad fruit. A tree is known by the kind of fruit it produces. You snakes! You are evil people, so how can you say anything good? The mouth speaks the things that are in the heart. Good people have good things in their hearts, and so they say good things. But evil people have evil in their hearts, so they say evil things."

Matthew 12:33–35

Dearest child,

ay attention to the words you speak today. Your words are the evidence of your heart, for the mouth speaks the things that are in the heart. As the fruit of a tree tells what kind of tree it is, your words will tell what kind of person you are inside. Whatever you have stored up in your secret self will be revealed by what you are saying to those around you. Your words have the power to crush or restore, to tear down or build up, to demoralize or encourage. When you are filled to overflowing with my Holy Spirit, your words cannot help but be a blessing to others. Jesus said, "The words I told you are spirit, and they give life." Dwell on his words so that the words which overflow from you may also be life-giving. Speak a blessing to someone today.

Your Father,
God

YOU HONOR ME WHEN YOU REST

"You must obey God's law about the Sabbath
   and not do what pleases yourselves on
      that holy day.
You should call the Sabbath a joyful day
   and honor it as the Lord's holy day.
You should honor it by not doing whatever
      you please
   nor saying whatever you please on that
      day.
Then you will find joy in the Lord."

Isaiah 58:13–14

"Remember to keep the Sabbath holy.
Work and get everything done during six
days each week, but the seventh day is a day
of rest to honor the Lord your God. On that
day no one may do any work: not you, your
son or daughter, your male or female slaves,
your animals, or the foreigners living in your
cities. The reason is that in six days the
Lord made everything—the sky, the earth,
the sea, and everything in them. On the
seventh day he rested. So the Lord blessed
the Sabbath day and made it holy."

Exodus 20:8–11

Dear child of mine,

Has it ever occurred to you that even I rested on the seventh day! Do you think that I was tired? The God of all power and might? The God of unfathomable strength? No, I rested on the seventh day so that you would see and understand that rest is part of the rhythm of my creation. It is woven into the fabric of my plan. It is my commandment for you.

Turn your heart toward me and delight in my Sabbath. If you honor me by ceasing from your own drivenness, by turning away from your own restless pursuits to spend time with me, you will discover my joy!

Rest in me.

God

WHY DO YOU QUESTION MY DESIGN?

"How terrible it will be for those who argue
    with the God who made them.
  They are like a piece of broken pottery
    among many pieces.
The clay does not ask the potter,
  'What are you doing?'
The thing that is made doesn't say to its
    maker,
  'You have no hands.' "

Isaiah 45:9

Dear child of mine,

here are still some things about yourself that you have not accepted. You view your abilities and assets with harsh and critical eyes and keep a constant record of your "limitations." You murmur and say, "I was made this way, but I should have been made that way!" or "If only I could be like this person or that person!"

Why do you insist on being your own worst enemy? Why do you question the judgment of the God who made you as you are? Does the clay say to the potter, "What are you doing? How dare you shape me this way?" No, the clay does not give advice to the potter. And neither are you to resist my design for your life.

I, your God and your Creator, have fashioned you for my purposes. Humble your heart. Embrace my way. Give thanks.

Your own
God

COME FORTH AND LIVE!

I felt the power of the Lord on me, and he brought me out by the Spirit of the Lord and put me down in the middle of a valley. It was full of bones. . . . He said to me, "Prophesy to these bones and say to them, 'Dry bones, hear the word of the Lord. This is what the Lord God says to the bones: I will cause breath to enter you so you will come to life. . . . Then you will know that I am the Lord.' "

So I prophesied as I was commanded. While I prophesied, there was a noise and a rattling. The bones came together, bone to bone. . . . And the breath came into them, and they came to life and stood on their feet, a very large army.

Then he said to me . . . "I will put my Spirit inside you, and you will come to life. Then I will put you in your own land. And you will know that I, the Lord, have spoken and done it."

Ezekiel 37:1–14

He saves my life from the grave
and loads me with love and mercy.

Psalm 103:4

My own dear child,

*A*re you going through a dry, desert time? Has your hope evaporated? Do you feel cut off from me and from others? Does your spirit feel more dead than alive? Listen to me now, my child. On your own you have no power to revive yourself—no power to bring life. But what you do have is the power to choose. You can choose today to call upon my name. You can choose to receive a new beginning from my hand. When you call, I will hear you. I will open the grave of your despair. I will bring you back to the land of the living. And then you will know that I am the Lord, the God who rescues you from the grave. I will put my Spirit in you, and you will live. I will settle you in the land of your spiritual inheritance. And you will bear testimony to all who ask that I, the Lord your God, have done it!

Come forth and live!
God

Praising Me Can Heal You

My whole being, praise the Lord;
    all my being, praise his holy name . . .
    and do not forget all his kindnesses.
He forgives all my sins
    and heals all my diseases. . . .
He satisfies me with good things
    and makes me young again, like the
        eagle. . . .
The Lord shows mercy and is kind.
    He does not become angry quickly,
        and he has great love. . . .
He has taken our sins away from us
    as far as the east is from west. . . .
But the Lord's love for those who respect
        him
    continues forever and ever.

Psalm 103:1–17

My dear child,

id you know that praising me can heal you? It can still your restless spirit and fill your empty soul. Turn to me and bring me praise. Let it spring from deep within your inmost being. Let your song exalt my holy name.

Remember my mercies and all of my benefits, for I am the God who heals and forgives. I am the Father who redeems your life and satisfies you with good things. I make you young again, like the eagle. Praise me, for I am slow to anger and abounding in love. I remove your sins as far from you as the east is from the west. Praise me, for my love continues forever. Turn to me and bring me praise.

I am the Lord, your
God

COME AWAY FROM THE COMFORTABLE

As Jesus was walking by Lake Galilee, he saw two brothers, Simon (called Peter) and his brother Andrew. They were throwing a net into the lake because they were fishermen. Jesus said, "Come follow me, and I will make you fish for people." So Simon and Andrew immediately left their nets and followed him.

Matthew 4:18–20

Then a teacher of the law came to Jesus and said, "Teacher, I will follow you any place you go."

Jesus said to him, "The foxes have holes to live in, and the birds have nests, but the Son of Man has no place to rest his head."

Matthew 8:19–20

When Jesus heard this, he said to him, "There is still one more thing you need to do. Sell everything you have and give it to the poor, and you will have treasure in heaven. Then come and follow me." But when the man heard this, he became very sad, because he was very rich.

Luke 18:22–23

My child,

Are you fashioning for yourself a life of comfort—a place where you can run away from reality?

Listen. Do you hear it? Somewhere on the margins of your comfort zone there is a voice crying out to you—a voice too persistent to ignore.

"Follow me," it keeps saying. "Follow me. Come away from the safe and the comfortable, the predictable and the socially correct. Follow me into a life of risk and challenge and high adventure, where the cost will be great but the rewards will be greater. Follow me, and I will make your existence count for more than comfort. I will lead you on narrow paths, up steep and rugged roads, into dangerous terrain. But I will give you weapons for the battle. I will fight beside you. And you will share my victory!"

Come away and follow!
God

You Are a Portrait in Progress

Our faces, then, are not covered. We all show the Lord's glory, and we are being changed to be like him. This change in us brings ever greater glory, which comes from the Lord, who is the Spirit.

2 Corinthians 3:18

Dearest child,

I am constantly working in your life—adding this color, that shadow, this line. Like an artist with a paintbrush, I am making you into the very image of my beautiful and sinless Son.

Don't constantly question what I am doing. Don't struggle against my hand. Learn to trust the Artist who stands back and sees from his own perspective what is needed in the portrait he is creating.

If you must question something today, ask this: "How will the circumstances of this day make me more like Jesus?" Then thank me for those circumstances and receive my grace to walk through them. I love you with a tenderness you cannot imagine.

Your Abba,
God

Return to Me

The Lord spoke his word to me, saying:
"Go and speak to the people of Jerusalem,
saying: This is what the Lord says:
   'I remember how faithful you were to me
      when you were a young nation.
   You loved me like a young bride.
   You followed me through the desert,
      a land that had never been planted.' "

Jeremiah 2:1–2

Dear child of mine,
remember the excitement of your early faith—the way you loved
me, the way you followed so trustingly as I led you to the other side
of that "desert time" you were going through. Always your first
thoughts were of me. I was never far from your heart back then. You
gave me the first fruits of your time, your energy, your attention. You needed me, and
I was there for you.

Where are you today? I haven't moved. I am still here, longing to spend time
with you.

Your loving Father,
God

CRY OUT TO ME

The blind man cried out, "Jesus, Son of David, have mercy on me!"

The people leading the group warned the blind man to be quiet. But the blind man shouted even more, "Son of David, have mercy on me!"

Jesus stopped and ordered the blind man to be brought to him. When he came near, Jesus asked him, "What do you want me to do for you?"

He said, "Lord, I want to see."

Jesus said to him, "Then see. You are healed because you believed."

Luke 18:38–42

Dear child,

ry out to me. Ask me what you will. Do not let others discourage you or dissuade you from seeking what you need from me. Be specific. Tell me exactly what you want me to do for you. And ask in the name of Jesus, my Son. (To ask in his name means to ask in accordance with his nature. I will not hear or respond to a request that is contrary to the nature of my incarnate Word, my Son.) Ask believing. Don't put your faith in faith, for faith in and of itself cannot help you. Instead, put your faith in me—in my willingness to heal and my power to change things.

Cry out boldly. Ask specifically. Use the name of Jesus. Have faith in me. And like the blind man of Jericho, you will receive what you need.

Mercifully,
God

The News Is Good

Praise be to the God and Father of our Lord Jesus Christ. In Christ, God has given us every spiritual blessing in the heavenly world. That is, in Christ, he chose us before the world was made so that we would be his holy people—people without blame before him. Because of his love, God had already decided to make us his own children through Jesus Christ. That was what he wanted and what pleased him, and it brings praise to God because of his wonderful grace. God gave that grace to us freely, in Christ, the One he loves. In Christ we are set free by the blood of his death, and so we have forgiveness of sins. How rich is God's grace, which he has given to us so fully and freely. God, with full wisdom and understanding, let us know his secret purpose. This was what God wanted, and he planned to do it through Christ. His goal was to carry out his plan, when the right time came, that all things in heaven and on earth would be joined together in Christ as the head.

Ephesians 1:3–10

My dear child,

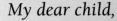ould you use a little good news today? Could you use a lot?
Then know these things: I have blessed you with every spiritual
blessing in the person of Jesus, my Son. I have held nothing back!
Every spiritual blessing that I possess is yours, in him.

I had my eye on who you would be long before I even created the world. You were
the one I wanted, the one I chose, to be holy—set apart for me! I knew way back then
that I wanted you for my child. This was my pleasure. This was my will. I desired to
pour out on you all the grace that I possess. And I did that very thing when I gave
you my Son as your Savior, your advocate, your friend. In Jesus you have everything!
Freedom through his blood. Forgiveness of sins. Full wisdom and understanding.

I've even revealed to you the mystery of my will. And this is it: I am going to
bring everything in heaven and earth together under one head, Jesus Christ. There
will be no more separation or sadness. Everything will be united in him.

When the stress and strain of your day starts getting to you, think about these
things. The news is good. Very good.

Your Creator and King,
God

Now You Belong!

You were not born Jewish. You are the people the Jews call "uncircumcised." Those who call you "uncircumcised" call themselves "circumcised." (Their circumcision is only something they themselves do on their bodies.) Remember that in the past you were without Christ. You were not citizens of Israel, and you had no part in the agreements with the promise that God made to his people. You had no hope, and you did not know God. But now in Christ Jesus, you who were far away from God are brought near through the blood of Christ's death.

Ephesians 2:11–13

My own,

nce you were on the outside, looking in. You were like a child whose nose is pressed against the window of a beautiful shop full of toys and candy, with no money to buy. You were like a child on the playground who longs to take part in the game but never gets picked to be on a team. You were like the foreigner who can't understand the language or traditions of the strange land he is traveling through. How lonely and lost he feels!

But now everything has changed. My Son has come for you. Now you belong; you are a part; you are on the inside! Jesus Christ has opened the door to the beautiful shop and has paid the price for your purchases. Jesus Christ has stopped the game and come over to you on the sidelines and has chosen you to be on his team. Jesus Christ has welcomed you into a new land where he is the King. He has taught you the language and the customs and made you a citizen. Now, at last, you are a member of the household of God!

Welcome, my child!

God

LOOK AT MY SON, THEN TURN TO ME

In your lives you must think and act like
Christ Jesus.
Christ himself was like God in everything.
But he did not think that being equal with
God was something to be used for his
own benefit.
But he gave up his place with God and made
himself nothing.
He was born to be a man
and became like a servant.
And when he was living as a man,
he humbled himself and was fully
obedient to God,
even when that caused his death—death
on a cross.

Philippians 2:5–8

Jesus answered, "I have been with you a
long time now. Do you still not know me,
Philip? Whoever has seen me has seen the
Father. So why do you say, 'Show us the
Father'?"

John 14:9

Dear one,

What do you know of a love like mine? A love that stoops to conquer? A love that reaches to redeem? Look at the life of my Son, and you will see my heart. I am the center and the soul of who he is, for he and I are one.

Look at him, the One who was willing to leave crowns and thrones and angels' praises to become a baby laid on straw. Look at him, the One who bowed to be baptized though he had never sinned. Look at him, the One who faced his own accusers, wordlessly accepting their sentence on his life. The One who bore abuse and torture, who bled and finally died so you could live to laugh and love and be reconciled to me.

All that you need to know of me, you will find in him.

Look at him. Look at my Son, your Savior.

Now, turn to me.

His Father and Yours,
God

BEGIN IN YOUR HEART

"How terrible for you, teachers of the law and Pharisees! You are hypocrites! You are like tombs that are painted white. Outside, those tombs look fine, but inside, they are full of the bones of dead people and all kinds of unclean things. It is the same with you. People look at you and think you are good, but on the inside you are full of hypocrisy and evil."

Matthew 23:27–28

My dear child,

*W*hen you bend all of your energy toward doing what is right and behaving as a good Christian should, the strain of your efforts will eventually show in your disposition. You will find yourself growing short-tempered with others—impatient with their flaws and errors. You will judge as less worthy than yourself anyone who seems less involved in striving for right behavior. And before you know it, your inner attitude will be saturated with the poison of pride.

This is exactly what happened to the Pharisees. They got so carried away with the rigid rules of external behavior that their hearts got far from me. On the outside, to the people on the street, they looked like perfection itself. But on the inside, where only I could see, they were filled with the rottenness of self-consciousness and pride. So don't begin with the outer you, striving to **do** holy things. Instead, begin in your heart by confessing that, apart from me, you are unable to be holy. Humbly lay down your own efforts at being "a good person" and let my Spirit fill you with my holiness, my goodness, my love.

You are so precious to me. I want to fill you with new life.

Your loving Father,

God

Use What Is Yours!

I pray also that you will have greater understanding in your heart so you will know the hope to which he has called us and that you will know how rich and glorious are the blessings God has promised his holy people. And you will know that God's power is very great for us who believe. That power is the same as the great strength God used to raise Christ from the dead and put him at his right side in the heavenly world.

Ephesians 1:18–20

Dearest child of mine,

Today if your banker called to tell you that someone had died and left you millions of dollars, how long would it take you to get dressed and down to the bank? You wouldn't leave the money there unclaimed and never write a single check on it, would you?

Well, I am telling you today that you have an inheritance worth far more than millions of dollars. It has already been deposited to your account—and yet you are not using it.

What is your inheritance? I have deposited to your spiritual account an unlimited supply of power. What kind of power? The exact same power that raised my Son Jesus Christ from the dead! The exact same power that seated him at my right hand here in heaven, high above all earthly rule, authority, power, or dominion! That is the kind of power that belongs to you when you believe in him.

Why do you sometimes go around with the attitude of a spiritual pauper? It is time to use what is yours. It is time to spend your inheritance for the spread of my kingdom.

Powerfully,
God

THANK ME FOR TRIALS

My brothers and sisters, when you have many kinds of troubles, you should be full of joy, because you know that these troubles test your faith, and this will give you patience. Let your patience show itself perfectly in what you do. Then you will be perfect and complete and will have everything you need.

James 1:2–4

Dear child,

*Y*ou may have thought that once you became a Christian all temptations and trials would disappear. Not so. Even Jesus was tempted, and he endured terrible trials. Temptations and trials are a part of your life while you are on this earth. They are also part of my plan for you. They force you to lean into my mercy and rely on my power. So don't resent them as enemies, but welcome them as friends! As they test your faith, they produce in you a valuable quality: endurance. And as this endurance becomes strong within you, you will find that you have gained the kind of spiritual maturity you never thought was possible—and all because of your trials and temptations. Thank me today for those trials and temptations, and trust me to overcome them in you through the power of my Holy Spirit!

Your Deliverer!

God

Bring Me the Things That Worry You

At that time Jesus said, "I praise you, Father, Lord of heaven and earth, because you have hidden these things from the people who are wise and smart. But you have shown them to those who are like little children. Yes, Father, this is what you really wanted.

"My Father has given me all things. No one knows the Son, except the Father. And no one knows the Father, except the Son and those whom the Son chooses to tell.

"Come to me, all of you who are tired and have heavy loads, and I will give you rest. Accept my teachings and learn from me, because I am gentle and humble in spirit, and you will find rest for your lives. The teaching that I ask you to accept is easy; the load I give you to carry is light."

Matthew 11:25–30

Dear child,

have hidden the treasures of my heart from the worldly wise and cynical, but I am revealing them now to you, for I see that you are willing to humble yourself and come to me like a child. What pleasure you give me when you are simple and trusting and childlike! Then, more than ever, I delight in you.

I am known to no one but my Son and those to whom he chooses to reveal my nature. When your heart is open to him, my heart is open to you!

Come now, bringing the things that worry or trouble you, the things that produce stress in your life. I did not create you to bear these things in your human strength. If you let me, I will carry them.

You have much to learn from Jesus. Spend time with him. You will find that his yoke is light and his burden is easy. This is the kind of load you were created to carry. Put on his gentleness and humility, and enter into my rest.

Come!

God

COME BELIEVING

Jesus said to the father, "You said, 'If you can!' All things are possible for the one who believes."

Immediately the father cried out, "I do believe! Help me to believe more!"

Mark 9:23-24

But if any of you needs wisdom, you should ask God for it. He is generous and enjoys giving to all people, so he will give you wisdom. But when you ask God, you must believe and not doubt. Anyone who doubts is like a wave in the sea, blown up and down by the wind. Such doubters are thinking two different things at the same time, and they cannot decide about anything they do. They should not think they will receive anything from the Lord.

James 1:5-8

My dear child,

When you need wisdom, come to me. I will supply it generously. But when you come, come believing, not doubting. The tiniest doubt splits the sails on your vessel of faith.

How do you handle the doubts that plague you? First of all, don't pretend. Be forthright with me. If you do have doubts, you cannot hide them from me, for I know you. Shine a flashlight on each small doubt that creeps, as an intruder, into your heart. Then ask me for help—for more faith. I will supply that, too. Learn to pray like this: "I do believe! Help me to believe more!"

There is no need to be tentative or shaky. I am your God. I know your heart and can heal your doubts. I supply faith and wisdom and guidance at every crossroad in your life.

Come believing!
God

Now, Share What You Have Been Given

Praise be to the God and Father of our Lord Jesus Christ. God is the Father who is full of mercy and all comfort. He comforts us every time we have trouble, so when others have trouble, we can comfort them with the same comfort God gives us. We share in the many sufferings of Christ. In the same way, much comfort comes to us through Christ.

2 Corinthians 1:3–5

Child of my kingdom,
here is someone very near you today who needs to know what you
know. Someone who needs a word of comfort or compassion or
encouragement.
When you were low, did someone lift you? When you were lost,
did someone help you find the way? I have allowed these difficult times in your life
so that you could experience my mercy.
And now someone else is going through a difficult time. Will you be the one to
bring my mercy, to share my comfort and guidance and encouragement? Will you
spread the light of my truth as one small candle spreads its light to another?
In this world, you are either part of the problem or part of the solution—part of
the darkness or part of the light. When you were engulfed in problems, someone
brought my merciful solution to you. When you had doubts and questions, someone
answered your questions with my healing and life-changing truth. Now it is time for
you to share what you have been given with someone in need. Will you reach out to
that someone today . . . for me?
Share my love.
God